DAVID L. SLOAN

PHANTOM PRESS
KEYWEST

© 2017 Phantom Press, Key West.

All materials contained are protected by international copyright laws and may not be reproduced, distributed, transmitted, displayed, published or broadcast without the prior written permission of David L. Sloan, Phantom Press, or in the case of third party materials, the owner of that content. Transgressors will be actively pursued and prosecuted by asshole iguanas. All images are owned or licensed.

You may not alter or remove any trademark, copyright or other notice from copies of the content.

For use of information contained as source material, credit: David L. Sloan, author, Iguanas Are Assholes.

Inquiries: david@phantompress.com

ISBN: 978-0-9831671-7-4

DEDICATED
TO
BJ & TWITCH

NO ANIMALS WERE HARMED IN THE MAKING OF THIS BOOK.

A PORTION OF THE AUTHOR'S PROCEEDS ARE
DONATED TO ANIMAL RESCUE ORGANIZATIONS.

DUE TO AN IGUANA STRIKE, SOME IMAGES OF IGUANAS
HAVE BEEN REPLACED WITH OTHER CREATURES.

IT SHOULD
BE DEDICATED
TO ME.

ASSHOLE

IGUANAS
ARE
ASSHOLES

IT
SHOULD
COME
AS
NO
SURPRISE
TO
YOU
THAT
IGUANAS
ARE
ASSHOLES.

AN ASSHOLE IGUANA
TRIED TO PUT BABY
IN A CORNER.

AN ASSHOLE IGUANA
EATS MY KIBBLE AND
MAKES MY TUMMY
GROWL LIKE A BEAR.

AN IGUANA ATE MY WIFE'S
FINGER AND NOW SHE CAN'T
PLAY FRISBEE.

IT IS SAFE TO SAY
IGUANAS ARE ASSHOLES.

LIZARDS AROSE FROM AMPHIBIANS ABOUT 320 MILLION YEARS AGO IN THE SWAMPS OF THE LATE CARBONIFEROUS.

ONCE ABLE TO WALK, THEY
PROCEEDED TO THE NEAREST
PATIO AND CRAPPED
ALL OVER IT.

BECAUSE IGUANAS ARE ASSHOLES.

ASSHOLE

YOU PROBABLY HATE
IGUANAS BECAUSE
THEY EAT ALL OF
YOUR SEXY FLOWERS
JUST AS THEY ARE
ABOUT TO BLOOM.

BUT AS FAR AS IGUANAS BEING ASSHOLES GOES... THAT BARELY QUALIFIES AS AN ASSHOLE MANEUVER

**IGUANAS INTENTIONALLY
POOP ON THE PATH WHERE
YOU INTEND TO WALK.**

**THEN THEY HIDE
IN NEARBY BUSHES
WITH THEIR FRIENDS
AND WAIT.**

WHEN
YOU STEP
IN THEIR POOP,
THEY LAUGH
AND LAUGH
AND LAUGH.
THEN
THEY HEAD OFF
TO EAT MORE OF
YOUR GARDEN
SO THEY CAN
POOP IN YOUR
PATH SOME
MORE.

IGUANAS
ARE
ASSHOLES!

IGUANAS HAVE A STOCKY STATURE.

A CLOSE INSPECTION OF THEIR SKIN WILL REVEAL THAT IT IS MADE OF ASSHOLE.

SOME HAVE SPINES
THAT PROTRUDE
FROM THEIR HEADS, NECKS,
BACKS AND TAILS.

**ARCHEOLOGISTS BELIEVE
THIS IS DUE TO THE FACT
THAT THEY ARE ASSHOLES.**

THE GREEN IGUANA CAN GROW UP TO 7 FEET IN LENGTH.

THAT IS A LOT OF ASSHOLE!

DID YOU KNOW THAT
IGUANAS USE THEIR TAILS
AS A WEAPON TO PUNCH
THINGS THEY DON'T LIKE?

ONLY AN ASSHOLE WOULD DO THAT.

OR MY SISTER

IGUANAS CAN ALSO DROP THEIR TAILS WHEN THEY ARE GRABBED BY A PREDATOR.

THE DETATCHED TAIL
WIGGLES AROUND TO
DISTRACT THE PREDATOR
WHILE THE ASSHOLE
IGUANA RUNS AWAY LIKE A
LITTLE SISSY.

GO AHEAD AND
RUN YA BIG SISSY!

NOTHING WORSE THAN A LITTLE SISSY ASSHOLE.

IGUANAS ALSO
HAVE A DEWLAP

A DEWLAP IS A FLAP OF LOOSE SKIN HANGING AROUND AN ANIMAL'S NECK.

NOT TO BE CONFUSED WITH AN MMMBOP.

THAT IS A HANSON SONG

COWS HAVE A DEWLAP
TOO, BUT COWS ARE CUTE
BECAUSE THEY HAVE FUR.

IGUANAS SIT AROUND ALL SCALEY WITHOUT FUR OR FEATHERS THINKING THEY ARE COOL OR SOMETHING.

I ROCK

BUT THEY ARE STILL ASSHOLES.

FURLESS, FEATHERLESS ASSHOLES.

SAVE THE SCALES. LOSER.

DID YOU KNOW IGUANAS HAVE A 3RD EYE?

NO, NOT THEIR ASSHOLE.

THE PARIETAL EYE IS LOCATED ON TOP OF THEIR HEADS AND REGULATES CIRCADIAN RHYTHMICITY.

I'VE GOT
RHYTHM

JUST LIKE
HALL & OATES

THESE ASSHOLES ARE WATCHING YOUR EVERY MOVE.

AND THEY ARE TOUGH
MOTHERFLUPPERS.

IGUANAS CAN FALL FROM HEIGHTS UP TO 50 FEET AND NOT GET INJURED.

I SEE THESE ASSHOLE
IGUANAS ARE GETTING
YOU PRETTY ANGRY. HERE
IS SOMETHING TO HELP
YOU CALM DOWN.

RANDOM PUPPY IN A SUITCASE

**YOU CAN ALSO CALM
YOURSELF DOWN BY
WRITING A HAIKU.**

DO NOT WORRY,
NOBODY REMEMBERS
HOW TO WRITE A HAIKU.

DEMENTIA

5 SYLLABLES
7 SYLLLABLES
5 SYLLABLES

Roses are red,
violets are blue,
if the truth be known,
I can't stand you.

**BUT YOU CAN
WRITE A POEM OR
A FREESTYLE RAP INSTEAD.**

**IF YOU ARE
READING
THIS BOOK IN
THE BATHROOM,
PEOPLE
ARE PROBABLY
STARTING TO
WONDER WHERE
YOU ARE,
SO TRY TO
WRAP THINGS UP.**

UNLESS YOU LIVE ALONE.
IF YOU LIVE ALONE,
TAKE YOUR TIME AND
ENJOY THESE
FASCINATING FACTS
ABOUT IGUANAS.

IGUANA
MOTHERS
ABANDON
THEIR
IGUANA
BABIES
BEFORE
THEY
ARE
BORN.

TOTAL ASSHOLE MOVE.

THEY CAN ALSO SWIM BETTER THAN MOST HUMANS, INCLUDING MICHAEL PHELPS

AND WE ALL KNOW, ONLY AN ASSHOLE CAN SWIM BETTER THAN MICHAEL PHELPS.

OLYMPICS ARE
STUPID

IGUANAS CAN SURVIVE 28 MINUTES UNDERWATER WITHOUT BREATHING.

BUT IGUANAS ARE NOT ALONE WITH THIS TALENT. AN ASSHOLE CAN SURVIVE 28 MINUTES UNDERWATER WITHOUT BREATHING TOO.

IGUANAS CAN ALSO INFLATE THEMSELVES TO FLOAT DURING A FLOOD

"TAKE THAT GOD!"
THEY SAY, FLIPPING OFF
NOAH AND HIS ARK.

IGUANAS ARE ASSHOLES OF BIBLICAL PROPORTIONS.

AND AS IF TO MOCK THE BIBLE EVEN MORE, SOME IGUANAS CAN WALK ON WATER.

THEY HAVE TO BE GOING PRETTY FAST, BUT STILL... WHAT ASSHOLES.

WE RAN OUT OF THINGS TO SAY 59 PAGES AGO. NICE TO SEE YOU ARE STILL READING.

AS LONG AS YOU ARE STILL HERE, HOW ABOUT A JOKE?

THE JOKE IS IN
YOUR HAND

WHAT DID
THE IGUANA
SAY TO THE
THREE-LEGGED SKUNK?

NOTHING.
ANIMALS CAN'T TALK.

WHAT DO YOU CALL AN IGUANA WITH A CARROT IN EACH EAR?

ANYTHING YOU WANT.
HE CAN'T HEAR YOU.

WHY DID THE IGUANA PUSH THE CAT INTO THE RIVER?

BECAUSE IGUANAS
ARE ASSHOLES.

WHAT DO YOU CALL AN IGUANA WHO BRINGS YOU FLOWERS?

HOW MANY IGUANAS
CAN YOU FIT
IN A BATH TUB?

WHAT DO YOU CALL AN IGUANA THAT SINGS WITH SNOOP DOGG?

DID YOU HEAR ABOUT THE OLD IGUANA WHO COULDN'T CHANGE COLOR?

BECAUSE IGUANAS HAVE ISSUES
ONLY A CHIROPRACTOR CAN FIX,
PLUS THEY HAVE GREAT BOOKS
IN THE WAITING ROOM.

BUT
ENOUGH
WITH
THE
AWESOME
JOKES.
WE
DON'T
WANT
TO
BREAK
ANY
FUNNY
BONES
HERE.

WE NEED TO TALK ABOUT BABY IGUANAS.

BABY IGUANAS ARE ASSHOLES TOO.

IN FACT, THEY EAT GROWN UP IGUANA'S POOP.

YET, IT IS OKAY TO FEEL SORRY FOR THEM.

IGUANAS IN CAPTIVITY HAVE BEEN KNOW TO KILL THEMSELVES IF NOT PROPERLY CARED FOR.

YOU WOULD PROBABLY DO
THE SAME IF YOUR ONLY
COMPANY WAS YOU AND
YOU WERE AN ASSHOLE.

BUT LET'S VISUALIZE A HAPPY THOUGHT...

HANGING OUT IN TIAJUANA

EATING BARBEQUED IGUANA.

NOW YOU WILL
PROBABLY HAVE THE SONG
"MEXICAN RADIO"
BY
WALL OF VOODOO
STUCK IN YOUR HEAD FOR
THE REST OF THE DAY.

YOU ARE WELCOME.

BUT THEY REALLY DO EAT THEM.

GO VEGAN

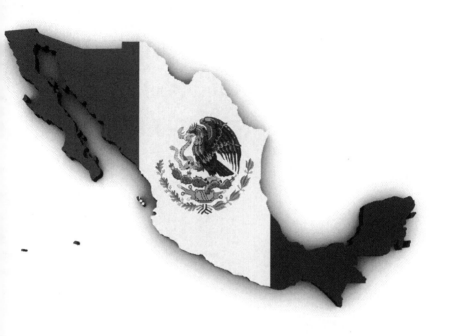

IGUANA MEAT HAS
HISTORICALLY BEEN
IMPORTANT IN THE CULINARY
TRADITIONS OF MEXICO AND
CENTRAL AMERICA.

PARTICULARLY IN THE STATES OF JALISCO, MICHOACAN AND COLIMA.

PROPER PREPARATION OF AN IGUANA REQUIRES PARBOILING IT IN SALTWATER FOR 20 MINUTES OR SO BEFORE ROASTING OR STEWING IT.

MEXICO PREFERS THE TASTE OF
THE GREEN IGUANA OVER THE
BLACK IGUANA, BUT THEY EAT
BOTH.

WOULD YOU LIKE AN IGUANA RECIPE?

TRY GOOGLE DUMMY.

AND NEVER FORGET THAT IGUANAS ARE ASSHOLES.

EAT MY BUTT

IT IS TRUE.

BUT IT SHOULD BE POINTED OUT
THAT IGUANAS THINK HUMANS
ARE ASSHOLES TOO.

**AND THEY ARE
PROBABLY RIGHT.**

HERE IS
A PHOTO OF
A PANDA BEAR.
SHE THINKS
IGUANAS ARE
ASSHOLES TOO.

SO DOES THIS GIRAFFE

ROOSTERS ARE ASSHOLES TOO.

ROBONEAL.com

STAY
TUNED

FOR A

VERY IMPORTANT

ABOUT THE AUTHOR

David L. Sloan is a begrudging iguana enthusiast. He lives in Islamorada, Florida near a natural iguana colony. Sloan used to tour as an iguana hypnotist on the carnival circuit, performing as Iguana Dave & The Traveling Lizard Show.

YOU
SMELL

Made in the USA
Columbia, SC
04 November 2019

82630917R00061